Akiko and Amy Part 1

I Talk You Talk Press

CONTENTS

1. AKIKO AND AMY

Akiko was bored. All her work was finished. The apartment was clean. The laundry and ironing were done. It was too early to cook food for her husband. He would not come home until about 9:00pm. It was 3:00pm now. After her marriage, Akiko had come to live in this small city. She didn't have any friends here and she was lonely.

She looked out the window. The American woman was parking her car. The Americans had moved into the apartment across the hall two weeks ago. The man went to work every morning, but the woman stayed home. Akiko loved speaking English. She was very interested in the new people. She wanted to talk to the woman but she was too shy.

Akiko watched the tall, light brown-haired woman take three supermarket bags and a big box out of the car. The woman dropped one of the bags. The bag broke. Potatoes and oranges rolled on the concrete.

Akiko ran to the door of her apartment. She took her eco bag from the hook and hurried down the stairs. Outside, the woman was kneeling on the ground. She was picking up the oranges and potatoes.

"Can I help you?" asked Akiko.

The woman smiled. "Thank you!"

Akiko knelt down. Together they put all the fruit and vegetables into Akiko's bag.

"I will carry the bags for you," said Akiko.

"Would you?" said the woman. "You are very kind."

"No problem," answered Akiko.

The tall woman carried the big box and Akiko carried the bags.

They climbed the stairs. When they got to the door of the Americans' apartment, the woman said,

"I'm Amy. Will you come in? I want to give your bag back."

"OK. My name is Akiko."

The Americans' apartment was the same as Akiko's but it looked different. There were books everywhere. Akiko thought it looked like an office.

Amy put the big box on the floor and they took the shopping bags and Akiko's eco bag into the kitchen.

"Do you have time for coffee?" asked Amy.

"Yes. That would be nice," answered Akiko.

"Please sit down," said Amy.

Akiko sat on a chair next to the table. She had never seen so many books in an apartment. There were two computers and a lot of paper as well.

Amy gave Akiko a big mug of coffee. She put a plate with muffins on it on the table.

"Please try one," said Amy. She sat down on the other side of the table.

Akiko took a muffin and ate a little. It was delicious.

"Are you a student?" Akiko asked Amy.

"No. I am writing a book."

"A book!" Akiko was interested. "A textbook for English?"

"No, no. I am writing a textbook. But it is history textbook. It's for American university students. It's about Boston."

"Bos – ton," said Akiko slowly. "That's in the United States?"

"Yes. Boston is my home town. When I finish the book, I will hunt for a job. Maybe a job teaching English. But these days I stay home every day. I find it very quiet, and sometimes I'm bored."

"I want you to teach me English," Akiko said quickly.

Amy didn't say anything. She looked at Akiko.

"I don't want to be your teacher," she said.

Akiko felt bad. She wanted to cry.

"I will pay you," she said quietly.

Amy touched Akiko's hand.

"I'm sorry," she said. "I hope to have some private English students, but not you."

"I'm sorry. I shouldn't have asked. I know my English is bad. But I want to learn to speak English better." Akiko wanted to run away.

Amy spoke again. "No. You are my neighbour. I don't want you to be my student. I hope you will be my friend. I hope we can do things together. Then we can speak English."

"Do things?" asked Akiko.

Amy smiled. "I don't know. What do you like to do? Maybe we could go shopping. Or maybe you could be a tour guide for me. I haven't been sightseeing yet. I like cooking. Maybe we can cook together."

Suddenly Akiko felt excited. "I want to be your friend."

"I am busy tomorrow. But I have free time the day after tomorrow. How about you?" asked Amy. "Are you free?"

"Yes," said Akiko. "I have free time most weekdays."

"Great! What shall we do?"

"Will you teach me…" Akiko laughed. "No, no. Not English! Will you teach me how to make muffins? These are delicious."

Amy laughed too. "Sure! It's a date."

2. AKIKO AND AMY MAKE MUFFINS

On Wednesday Akiko went shopping. She wanted to buy a present for her new friend Amy. Amy was going to teach Akiko how to make muffins. Amy and Akiko had a date for 11:00am, Thursday.

Akiko didn't know what to buy. She didn't know Amy well. She had met Amy on Tuesday for the first time.

What do American women like? she wondered.

Then she had a good idea. *I will buy her some coffee. We will make muffins. We will drink coffee and eat muffins.*

On Thursday morning, Akiko rang the bell of Amy's apartment.

"Come in. The door isn't locked," said Amy.

Amy was in the kitchen. Akiko gave her the coffee.

"Thank you!" said Amy. "We can drink this coffee when we eat the muffins. Let's start cooking."

"What shall I do?" asked Akiko.

"First we need to turn the oven on," said Amy. "The temperature should be 180. Do you have an oven like mine?"

"Yes," answered Akiko. "The size is almost the same."

Amy took two cake pans from the cupboard. "These are muffin pans. In America, our ovens are much bigger. So I can put two pans in the oven. In Japan, my oven is small so we will only put one pan in at a time. First we have to prepare the pans."

Amy picked up a spray can and sprayed a little into each space in the muffin trays.

"What's that?" asked Akiko.

"It's cooking oil", said Amy. "But you can put a little margarine or butter on a paper towel and use that."

Next, Amy put flour, baking powder, sugar, eggs, milk and butter on the table.

"What flavour muffins do you like?" asked Amy.

"I don't know," answered Akiko. "What flavours do you have?"

"We can have chocolate or blueberry today. I have cocoa and I have frozen blueberries. What would you like?"

"Oh, chocolate please," said Akiko.

Amy took cocoa and chocolate chips from the cupboard.

"Now we can start," she said.

Amy told Akiko to put two cups of flour, half a cup of sugar, half a cup of cocoa and 20ml of baking powder into a big bowl. Then Akiko mixed everything together very well using a big whisk.

"This cocoa doesn't look like the cocoa in my house," said Akiko.

"I guess that you have drinking chocolate or drinking cocoa. Drinking cocoa has milk powder and maybe sugar in it. For cooking we need pure cocoa," explained Amy.

Amy added half a cup of chocolate chips to the bowl.

"Now we'll put 100 grams of butter into a pot. We'll put in on the gas and wait till it melts. We don't want a high gas flame. The butter might burn."

Akiko put the butter in a pot. She put the pot on the range and turned on the gas. Soon the butter was melted and Amy added one cup of milk and one egg. She gave the pot to Akiko. Akiko mixed the butter, the milk and the egg together.

Then Amy gave Akiko a big spoon and said, "Add the liquids from the pot to the big bowl. Use this spoon to mix, but only mix a little."

Akiko added the egg, butter and milk to the big bowl and started to stir with spoon.

"Stop!" said Amy loudly.

Akiko jumped. She was surprised. "Oh, sorry. Am I doing the wrong thing?"

"No, no. It's OK. But you only mix muffins a little."

"But the mixture is not smooth," said Akiko.

"No. It's lumpy isn't it? That's OK. If muffins are mixed too much, they are not so good."

Akiko and Amy put muffin mix into each hole in the muffin pans. Then they put the first pan in the oven. Amy set the timer for 15 minutes.

Akiko was worried. Her muffin mixture did not look nice. It was not smooth. She thought her first muffins would not taste good. After 15 minutes, Amy took the muffin pan out of the oven. She put the second pan in the oven and set the timer.

"Look what you made!" she said to Akiko. There were six beautiful muffins. They had tops like little mountains.

Akiko and Amy drank coffee and ate a muffin. The muffins tasted great!

"Thank you very much," said Akiko.

"You're welcome," said Amy. "You said you haven't made muffins before. But I can tell you are a very good cook."

"I should be," said Akiko. "After high school I went to cooking school. I wanted to be a chef."

"Why aren't you a chef?" asked Amy.

"I met my husband, before I graduated. As soon as I graduated we got married and came here."

"Why don't you get a chef's job here?" asked Amy.

Akiko didn't answer. She didn't think that Amy would understand.

Amy looked at Akiko. *Akiko is very nice,* she thought. *But I don't think she is happy. I wonder why she doesn't get a job.*

"Why don't you take some muffins home for your husband?"

"Can I?" asked Akiko. "That would be great! My husband loves chocolate. I will buy some muffin pans. Then I can make muffins when my husband's mother comes. She doesn't think I cook well."

"But you are a trained chef!" Now Amy was surprised.

"I am sure you cook very well," said Amy. "I hope sometime soon you will teach me how to cook some Japanese food."

"Oh, yes!" smiled Akiko. "I can do that. But I have another plan for our next meeting. Do you like Ukiyo-e?"

"I don't know," said Amy. "I don't know what it is."

"Hmmm. I don't know how to say it in English. They are pictures. Like art. Old Tokyo."

"I love art," said Amy.

"Good! Are you free next week? There will be many ukiyo-e in the city museum. It is a special event."

"Any day is OK for me," said Amy.

"Can we go on Wednesday in the morning?" asked Akiko. "Then if you have free time, we can eat lunch."

6

"Sounds great!" answered Amy. I'll see you next Wednesday morning. What time?"

"Ten o'clock?" asked Akiko.

"Yes. Ten o'clock is fine. I'll be ready."

3. AKIKO AND AMY LOOK AT UKIYO-E

On Wednesday morning, Amy knocked on the door of Akiko's apartment. Akiko opened the door.

"Good morning," said Akiko.

"Hi," said Amy. "Are you ready to go out?"

"Yes." Akiko put on her shoes and picked up her bag. She locked the door and the two women walked downstairs.

"How do we get to the art museum?" asked Amy.

"We can take a bus from the bus stop opposite the supermarket," answered Akiko.

It was a beautiful day. It was a little cold, but the sky was blue and there were no clouds.

When Amy and Akiko reached the bus stop, Akiko read the timetable. "There should be a bus in about three minutes," she said.

"Good timing!" laughed Amy. "How much will the bus cost?"

"I don't know," answered Akiko. "When we get on the bus, we take a ticket. It has a number on it. At the front of the bus there is a display. When we get off the bus, we look at the display. It will tell us how much money to pay."

"OK. I understand," said Amy.

The art museum was not crowded. Amy and Akiko did not have to wait in line to buy an entrance ticket to see the ukiyo-e. The tickets were 500 yen.

Inside the display room, most of the ukiyo-e were hung on the walls. There were also some glass cases with security guards next to them.

Amy walked over to look at the first print.

"Now I know what ukiyo-e are," she said. "They are wood block prints."

"Uh," said Akiko. "Can you say that again?"

"Wood block prints." Amy spoke the words slowly. "They are very famous in western countries but I have never seen any original prints."

Akiko was interested. "Why do western people know about Japanese wood block prints?"

"Many famous western artists liked these Japanese ukiyo-e. They copied ideas from them and used them in their own paintings," explained Amy. "Do you know of Vincent Van Gogh or Monet?"

"Yes. I know the names," answered Akiko.

"Vincent van Gogh's paintings were influenced by Japanese ukiyo-e. In one of his paintings you can see ukiyo-e. And Monet collected more than 200 ukiyo-e. He loved Japanese things," explained Amy.

"Did van Gogh and Monet visit Japan?" asked Akiko.

"I don't think so. But they knew many people who had been to Japan. Let's look at some more." Amy moved to the next picture on the wall.

Akiko had a catalogue. It was all in Japanese so she was trying to translate some of it for Amy.

"This is number thirty-three," said Amy. What does it say in the book?"

Akiko was trying hard. "Uh. It says this is from Meiji times. It is by Hiroshige. He made eight prints of Mount Omi. This is one of them. "

"I like it," said Amy. "Would they have any of the Edo road ukiyo-e here? I would like to see those."

Akiko was puzzled. "I don't know what you mean." She looked quickly at all the pages in the guidebook. "There isn't anything about Edo road prints here."

"You know," said Amy. "There was a famous road and it had places where people stopped for a rest. I think there were fifty of them. A man made ukiyo-e of all the stops."

Akiko smiled. "You mean the Fifty Three Stations of the Tokaido! Tokaido was the road between Tokyo and Kyoto. Tokyo was called Edo then."

"Yes. That's what I mean. Are there any here?"

Akiko was pleased. "Yes. We can see a whole set of them. The same man who made this print made them. His name was Hiroshige."

Akiko and Amy enjoyed the display very much. They looked at everything. The ukiyo-e in the glass cases were very old. They were black and white. They had been made as pictures to go in books.

After Akiko and Amy had finished, they went to the coffee shop in the museum. They ate lunch. The lunchtime special was pasta, salad, coffee and dessert for 1,500 yen.

After lunch, they walked in the park near the art gallery. Amy asked Akiko the names of the trees but Akiko didn't know.

Amy is interested in everything, thought Akiko. *I will have to study a lot to answer her questions.*

4. MONSTER MOTHER-IN-LAW

Akiko and Amy met two or three times every week. Sometimes they drank coffee or cooked together, but usually they went out. They went shopping. They went to the movies. They went for bicycle rides. They always had fun.

One Wednesday, they were walking down the stairs. They were going to try a new noodle restaurant. An older woman was opening the door to her apartment. She stopped and looked at them. She said something in Japanese to Akiko. Akiko looked at her feet.

When they arrived at the restaurant, they sat at a table and looked at the menu. Akiko was very quiet. She was unhappy.

"What's wrong?" asked Amy. "What did the old woman say to you?"

Akiko was sad. "She is a friend of my mother-in law," she said. "Her name is Sato san. She is going to Okayama tomorrow. She will visit my mother-in-law. Sato san said that she will tell my mother-in-law that I am not a good wife."

"What does she mean?" Amy laughed.

"Sato san said I am always going out. I am always having fun. I am not staying at home and waiting for my husband."

Amy did not understand. "You are always home in the evening," she said. "Is your husband angry because you go out in the daytime?"

"No, no," answered Akiko. "My husband is happy. He listens to my stories and he laughs. He is a very nice man. He thinks a busy life is good for me."

"So what's the problem?" asked Amy.

"My mother-in-law is a monster," explained Akiko. "She doesn't like me. My husband and I were a love match. She wanted to find a wife for my husband. She said I would not be a good wife."

Amy thought Akiko was trying not to cry.

"Never mind," she said. "Your mother-in-law is in Okayama. Forget about it! Let's have a nice lunch."

Akiko tried hard. She tried to forget what Sato san had said. The restaurant cooked good food. Amy and Akiko had noodles and tea.

Amy had read about doctor fish on the Internet. Doctor fish are very small fish. They eat all the dead skin on your feet. It is like a pedicure. There was a beauty spa about 30 km away that had doctor fish. Amy wanted to try it.

"Let's go, Akiko," she said. "It will be fun!"

"OK," said Akiko. She didn't say anything to Amy but she was still very worried. She didn't want trouble with her mother-in-law.

Akiko and Amy made a plan to go to the beauty spa next Monday. They would leave early in the morning because Akiko always wanted to be home by 4:00pm. She cooked dinner for her husband and prepared his bath. Sometimes he came home at 6:00pm, but sometimes he came home very late. Akiko was always ready. Her apartment was very clean and she was a very good cook.

Amy thought Akiko was a very good wife.

Akiko and Amy never met on Saturdays or Sundays. But on Saturday morning, Akiko rang the bell of Amy's apartment. Amy's husband Dick answered the door. "Hello," he said. "Are you Akiko?"

"Yes," said Akiko.

"It's great to meet you," said Dick. "I'm Dick. Come in."

"I can't," answered Akiko. "Please tell Amy I can't go to try the doctor fish on Monday. My mother-in-law is arriving this morning. She will stay with us."

"Amy told me about the doctor fish." Dick laughed. "You should take your mother-in-law with you. She might enjoy it."

Amy looked at her feet. "I'm sorry. You don't understand. Please tell Amy. I have to go now."

5. THE MONSTER MOTHER-IN-LAW VISITS AKIKO

It was Wednesday. Amy was worried about Akiko. She hadn't seen her for a week. She thought about what had happened.

Last Wednesday, Akiko and Amy had met Sato san on the stairs. Sato san said she was going to Okayama. She would meet her friend. Sato san's friend was Akiko's mother-in-law. Sato san said that Akiko was always going out. She said she would tell Akiko's mother-in-law that Akiko did not look after her husband. She was a bad wife.

That day Akiko had been very unhappy.

On Saturday, Akiko's mother-in-law came from Okayama to stay with Akiko and her husband. Amy liked Akiko very much. She was sad because her friend was unhappy.

Amy asked her husband. "Dick. Do you think I should go to see Akiko? Maybe I can help her."

"No," answered Dick. "I think that would be a bad idea. I think it would make trouble for Akiko."

After Dick went to the university, Amy tried to write.

She was writing a book. It was hard work. Amy was thinking about Akiko. She wasn't thinking about her book.

The doorbell rang. Amy went to the door and opened it. It was Akiko.

"Come in. Come in," said Amy. She took Akiko's arm and pulled her into the apartment. Akiko sat down.

"How are you?" asked Amy.

"Terrible," answered Akiko.

Amy looked at her friend. Akiko did not look good.

"What's the problem?" asked Amy.

"My mother-in-law. She says everything I do is wrong. She says the apartment is not clean. She tells me to clean it again. I clean again. Then my mother-in-law says it is not clean enough."

"Why doesn't your mother-in-law clean the apartment?" asked Amy.

"She is too busy," answered Akiko. "She is cooking all the time. She is teaching me to cook."

"You are a great cook!" Amy was angry.

"My mother-in-law says that my cooking is not healthy."

"What does your husband say?" asked Amy?

Akiko smiled. "When his mother is not there, he tells me he likes my cooking. He doesn't like his mother's food. When his mother is there, he says that her food is delicious.

"My mother-in-law took all my husband's shirts and washed them again. She ironed them too. She said I do not wash and iron well!"

"I think your mother-in-law is crazy!" said Amy.

"No. She is not crazy. She loves her son very much but she doesn't like me."

"Where is your mother-in-law now?" asked Amy.

"She has gone shopping with Sato san. She told me to clean the windows while she was gone."

"When will your mother-in-law come back?" asked Amy.

"Oh, maybe two hours or three hours," answered Akiko.

"OK," said Amy. "I will come to your apartment and we will clean the windows together. It will be fun!"

Amy and Akiko cleaned windows together. They played Akiko's favourite music on the CD player. It was fun.

After one and a half hours Amy went home. The windows were very clean. Akiko sat down. She felt happy.

The next afternoon, Akiko went to Amy's apartment. She looked very happy.

"How are you?" asked Amy.

"I'm great!" said Akiko.

"Did your mother-in-law like our window cleaning?"

"She didn't look at the windows. She was very angry."

"Why?" asked Amy. Amy thought it was very strange. The monster mother-in-law was very angry, but Akiko was happy.

Akiko explained. "My mother-in-law and Sato san went shopping. After shopping, they went to a coffee shop. They were talking about me. I think they said bad things about me. Then Sato san said that my husband was very stupid to marry me.

"My mother-in-law didn't like Sato san to say her son was stupid. She was very angry. She came back to our apartment. She said she must go back to Okayama. She doesn't want to see Sato san! She caught the train this morning! Now when can we go to the spa to try the doctor fish?"

THANK YOU

Thank you for reading Akiko and Amy Part 1. (Word count: 3,803) We hope you enjoyed it. Akiko and Amy's story continues in part 2 and part 3.

If you would like to read more graded readers, please visit our website http://www.italkyoutalk.com

Other Level 3 graded readers include
A Dangerous Weekend
A Holiday to Remember
Akiko and Amy Part 2
Akiko and Amy Part 3
Be My Valentine
Different Seas
Enjoy Your Business Trip
Enjoy Your Homestay
I Need a Friend
Old Jack's Ghost Stories from England (1)
Old Jack's Ghost Stories from England (2)
Old Jack's Ghost Stories from Ireland
Old Jack's Ghost Stories from Japan
Old Jack's Ghost Stories from Scotland
Old Jack's Ghost Stories from Wales
Party Time!
Stories for Christmas

The Curse
Together Again
Who is Holly?

ABOUT THE AUTHOR

I Talk You Talk Press is a Japan-based publisher of language textbooks, graded readers and language learning/teaching resources.

Our team is made up of highly experienced language teachers and translators, who have all studied at least one additional language to an advanced level.

This experience enables us to design our materials from the perspective of both the teacher and the learner. We consult with both teachers and language learners when designing our textbooks and graded readers, and test our materials extensively in the classroom before publication.

We are a fast-growing press, and currently publish graded readers for learners of English. We publish new graded readers monthly.

Akiko and Amy Part 1